Julie Hasler's cross stitch projects

65 Quick & Easy Designs Perfect for Home, Children, and Special Occasions.

St. Martin's Griffin
New York

Dedication

To Calvin – a very special friend

Acknowledgements

I would like to thank the following people for their skilful sewing-up of the cross stitch embroideries: Stella Baddeley, Lesley Buckerfield, Joyce Formbey, Odette Coe, Maureen Hipgrave, Alison Mortley, Dawn Parmley, Lynda Potter and Jenny Whitlock; and to Connie Woolcott for the making-up of the projects. Also thanks to Janet Dobney, Hazel Nutting, Dawn Parmley, Lesley Smith and Brett Tucker for the design ideas. I would also like to thank the following companies who have contributed embroidery threads, fabrics, accessories and graph paper: DMC Creative World Ltd, and H.W. Peel & Co. Ltd.

The publishers would like to thank Jason Waterworth at Nice Irma's for kindly lending props for the photographs and Cara Ackerman at DMC for supplying materials.

Nice Irma's Ltd
46 Goodge Street
London W1P 1FJ
Tel: 0171 580 6921

First published in 1996 by
B.T. Batsford Ltd
4 Fitzhardinge Street
London W1H 0AH

Library of Congress Cataloging-in-Publication Data

Hasler , Julie S.
    Julie Hasler's cross stitch projects : 65 quick and easy projects
for home , children , and special occasions / by Julie Hasler.
        p.   cm.
    Includes index.
    ISBN 0-312-14973-5
    1. Cross-stitch-patterns. I. Title.
    TT778.C76H37337   1996
    746.44'3041--dc20   96-25837
                                                             CIP

First St. Martin's Griffin Edition : January 1997
10 9 8 7 6 5 4 3 2 1

Printed in Hong Kong

Photography by Marie-Louise Avery

Contents

Introduction

Cross stitch embroidery dates back thousands of years. The earliest examples depicted animals, mythological beasts, figures, flowers, fruit and scenes from nature. Cross stitch continued to be the most popular embroidery stitch for historical samplers throughout the centuries, and is today enjoying a strong resurgence. Needlecrafts are becoming increasingly popular among people of all age groups. More and more people are turning to the relaxing craft of cross stitch to personalize soft furnishings, linen and clothing.

Cross stitch is a very rewarding and inexpensive hobby; what's more, it is very easy to do. There are a few simple, basic rules to learn, but once you have mastered these, you can attempt any design. With a little practice, you will be able to achieve results that even an expert needle-woman would be proud of. Whether you are an experienced needleworker or still a beginner, this book offers a varied range of designs to suit your ability.

If you are a beginner, you will find the 'Getting Started' chapter very useful – it covers in detail the materials you will need for the projects, as well as explaining all the stitch techniques with step-by-step diagrams and instructions. There are also plenty of useful tips and advice on the aftercare of your embroidery.

The designs are grouped into three themes – Special Occasions, Children and the Home. Each chapter contains a wealth of full-colour charted designs. Project ideas are given with full instructions, but these are just suggestions. The designs are intended to be inspirational; you can add your own details – colour choices, mix-and-match borders and motifs – in order to create your own unique designs. The design possibilities are endless.

chapter one

Getting Started

This opening chapter lists the different materials required for getting started and explains the simple techniques involved. The basic stitches – cross stitch and back stitch – are shown in clear, step-by-step diagrams; as you can see, it really is very easy! At the end of the chapter I have put together a table of washing instructions so that you know how to look after your finished piece of embroidery. After reading all this, you will be well-equipped to start work on any number of the designs and projects in this book.

Materials

Needles

A small blunt tapestry needle (No. 24 or No. 26) is better than a conventional needle because it will pass neatly through the holes in the fabric without splitting the threads.

Fabric

Evenweave fabrics (such as Aida, Hardanger and Linda) are ideal for cross stitch as it is easy to count the threads. The fabrics are available in a wide choice of colours including white, ecru, black, red, blue, green and yellow. They also come in varying thread counts. Do not use a fabric without an even weave, as it will distort the embroidery either horizontally or vertically. The type of fabric required is stated within the directions for each project.

Threads

The designs in this book have been worked with DMC six-stranded embroidery cottons. A conversion chart is included on page 92. The number of strands you use depends upon the fabric you work on. Details are given with each project, but generally, three strands are used for 11-count fabric, two strands for 14-, 16- and 18-count fabric, and one strand for 22-count and finer work.

Embroidery Hoop

A round plastic or wooden hoop with a screw-type tension adjuster is ideal for cross stitch – 10 cm (4"), 12.5 cm (5") or 15 cm (6"). Bigger frame sizes are available for the larger designs. It is important to use a hoop that is large enough to fit the whole design inside – otherwise, if you have to move the hoop midway through working your embroidery, you risk distorting the stitches.

Scissors

Two pairs of scissors are required. A pair of sharp embroidery scissors are essential for unpicking or cutting out a mistake. A pair of large dressmaking scissors are used to cut the fabric. When cutting your fabric, make sure that you follow the line of the threads to ensure that you have a straight edge.

Preparing to work

There are two ways of preventing the edges of the fabric unravelling: you can cover them with a fold of masking tape or alternatively use whip-stitching or machine stitching.

Your first stitch is important as it will position the finished design on the fabric. You will need to find the centre point of the chart. To do this, count the width of the chart in squares, and then its length. Find the mid-point of each dimension and follow the grid lines towards the centre of the chart. The centre point is where these lines intersect. Next, locate the centre of your fabric by folding it in half vertically and then horizontally, pinching along the folds. If you prefer, mark along these lines with basting stitches. The centre stitch of your design will be where the folds in the fabric meet.

It is best to start stitching at the top of the design. To locate this position, count the squares up from the centre of the chart, then count left or right to the first symbol. Next, count the corresponding number of holes up and across from the centre of the fabric and begin at that point. Remember that each square on the chart represents a square on the fabric: i.e., one stitch.

To place the fabric in the embroidery hoop, put the area of fabric to be worked over the inner ring and gently push the outer ring over it. Gently and evenly pull the fabric, tightening the adjuster as you go, so that it is taut in the hoop and the mesh is straight. When working, you will find it easier to have the screw in the 'ten-o'clock' position to prevent your thread from becoming tangled. If you are left-handed, have the screw in the 'one-o'clock' position. You will need to re-tighten the fabric as you work. Tension makes stitching easier, enabling the needle to be pushed through the holes without piercing the fibres of the fabric.

When working with stranded cotton, always separate the strands and place them together again before threading your needle and beginning to stitch. Never double the thread. These simple steps will allow for much better coverage of the fabric and will give a neater finish.

Stitch techniques

Cross stitch

To begin the stitch, bring the needle up from the wrong side, through a hole in the fabric at the left end of a row of stitches of the same colour (Fig. 1). Fasten the thread by holding a short length of thread on the underside of the fabric, securing it with the first two or three stitches made, as in Fig. 2. Never use knots to fasten your thread as this will create a bumpy back surface and the finished piece of work will not lie flat.

Bring the needle across one square (or block) to the right and one square above on a left-to-right diagonal. Insert the needle as in Fig. 1. Half of the cross stitch is now completed. Continue in this way until you reach the end of the row. Your stitches should be diagonal on the right side of the fabric and vertical on the wrong side.

To complete the upper half of the stitch, cross back from right to left to form an 'X' (Fig. 3). Work all the stitches in the row (Fig. 4).

Alternatively, cross stitch can be worked by crossing each stitch as you come to it, as you would do for isolated stitches. This method works just as well; it is really a question of personal preference.

Work vertical rows of stitches as shown in Fig. 5. Finish all threads by running your needle under four or more stitches on the wrong side of the work (Fig. 6). Cut the thread close.

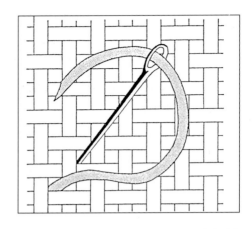

Fig. 1

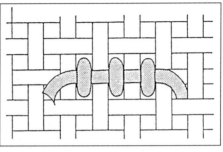

Fig. 2

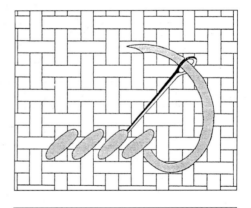

Fig. 3

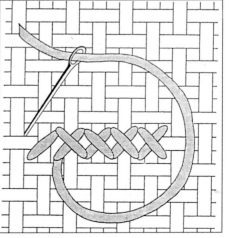

Fig. 4

Fig. 5

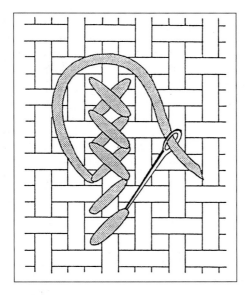

Fig. 6

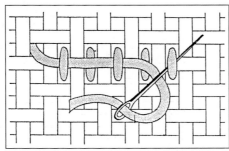

Fig. 7

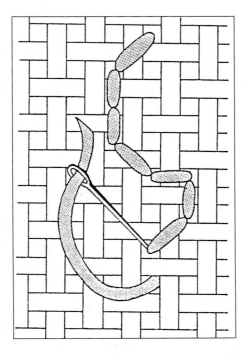

Basic backstitch

Backstitch is used in some of the designs in this book, mainly for outlines and finer details.

Work the backstitch once your cross stitch embroidery has been completed.

Always use one strand less than that used in the embroidery. For example, if three strands of stranded cotton have been used to work the cross stitch, use two strands for the backstitching. If only one strand is used for the cross stitch, use one strand for the backstitching.

Backstitch is worked from hole to hole and can be stitched in diagonal, vertical or horizontal lines (Fig. 7). Always take care not to pull the stitches too tight, otherwise the contrast of colour will be lost against the cross stitches. Finish off the threads as for cross stitch (Fig. 6).

Useful tips

1 Always wash your hands before starting work on your embroidery so that you don't soil the fabric or the threads.

2 Never leave food or plants near your embroidery.

3 Do not work on your embroidery wearing fluffy jumpers, and keep pets well away. Fluff and pet hairs can ruin your embroidery.

4 Ensure that you have enough thread to complete the project you are working on, as dye lots can vary.

5 When you are stitching, it is important not to pull the fabric out of shape. Work the stitches in two motions, straight up through a hole in the fabric and then straight down, making sure that the fabric remains taut. Pull the thread snug, but not too tight. If you follow this method, you will find that the thread lies just where you want it to and your fabric will not be pulled out of shape.

6 If your thread becomes twisted, drop your needle and let it hang down freely until it untwists itself. Do not continue working with twisted thread as it will appear thinner and cover your fabric less well.

7 Never leave your needle in the design area of your work when it is not in use. No matter how good the needle, it might rust and mark your work permanently.

8 Do not carry thread across an open expanse of fabric. If you are working separate areas of the same colour, finish off and begin again. Loose threads, especially dark colours, will be visible from the right side of your work when your project is completed.

9 Keep your work wrapped up when it is not in use. I find plastic carrier bags or pillowcases very useful for this.

10 When you have completed your cross stitch embroidery, it will need to be pressed. To protect your work, place the embroidery right-side down on to a soft towel and cover the reverse side with a thin, slightly damp cloth. Press with a hot iron.

Aftercare

You may find that at some stage your cross stitch projects will need to be laundered. This is no problem; just follow the simple advice which is specifically recommended by DMC in conjunction with their six-stranded cotton.

The following recommendations are for washing embroidery separately from all other laundry.

Cotton or Linen Fabric

Recommended Washing

Wash in soapy, warm water.
Rinse thoroughly.
Squeeze without twisting and hang to dry.
Iron on reverse side, under two layers of white linen.

Bleaching or Whitening Agent

Dilute according to the manufacturer's instructions.
Pre-soak the embroidery in clear water first, then soak for 5 minutes in a solution of 1 tablespoon of disinfectant per quart of cold water.
Rinse thoroughly in cold water.

Dry Cleaning

Avoid dry cleaning.
Some spot removers (benzene, trichlor-ethylene) can be used on small stains.

Synthetic Fabric

Recommended Washing

Washing is not recommended.

Bleaching or Whitening Agent

Follow instructions for cotton or linen if the white of the fabric is not of a high standard.
If the fabric is a pure white (white with a bluish tinge), do not use bleaching or whitening agent.

Dry Cleaning

Not recommended even for small stains.

chapter two

Designs for Special Occasions

This chapter contains a wealth of designs as well as gift ideas for friends and family, including projects for men. Here are designs for 18th and 21st Birthdays, Christmas, Easter, Engagement, Get Well, Birth of a New Baby, Anniversary, Good Luck, Mother's Day, Father's Day and Halloween. In addition to these, try to create your own projects. For example, the basket of fruit on page 19 is used on a Get Well card, but it would make a lovely motif for a sweatshirt. The signs of the Zodiac are shown in porcelain trinket boxes, but they would look equally good as birthday cards. Alternatively, sew all twelve designs as a Zodiac sampler or wall hanging.

Greetings cards

Personalized greetings cards with an embroidered design are a pleasure to make or to receive and a wonderful way of showing someone that you care. These cards will be treasured long after shop-bought ones have been forgotten or discarded.

Materials

Special occasion cards:

18th Birthday: 16 x 10 cm (6 ¼ x 4") DMC presentation card in pale pink with rectangular cut-out.
Birth of a Baby: 16 x 10 cm (6 ¼ x 4") DMC presentation card in pale pink with round cut-out.
Get Well Soon: 16 x 10 cm (6 ¼ x 4") DMC presentation card in pale blue with oval cut-out.
Good Luck: 16 x 10 cm (6 ¼ x 4") DMC presentation card in holly green with oval cut-out.
Christmas: 20 x 15 cm (7 ¾ x 5 ¾") Framecraft `craftacard' in white with rectangular cut-out.
Easter: 20 x 15 cm (7 ¾ x 5 ¾") Framecraft `craftacard' in white with oval cut-out.

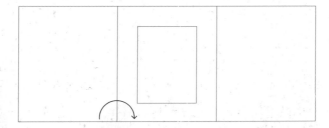

Pieces of fabric:

18th Birthday and Birth of a Baby: white Aida, 14 stitches to the inch
Get Well Soon: white Aida, 18 stitches to the inch
Good Luck: white Hardanger, 22 stitches to the inch
Christmas: sky-blue Aida, 18 stitches to the inch
Easter: white Aida, 14 stitches to the inch

DMC six-strand stranded embroidery cotton
Tapestry needles (No. 24 and No. 26)
Double-sided adhesive tape

Instructions

1   Work the cross stitch embroidery centrally onto your fabric, using two strands of stranded cotton throughout for the 14- and 18-count designs, and one strand for the 22-count.

2   When you have completed the cross stitch embroidery, press if required, then centre the design in the card window using the double-sided adhesive tape to fix the design into the card, pressing the backing down firmly.

Tip. You can economise on fabric by cutting a piece large enough to sew several designs (but remember to give each one enough space), rather than cutting a small piece for each design.

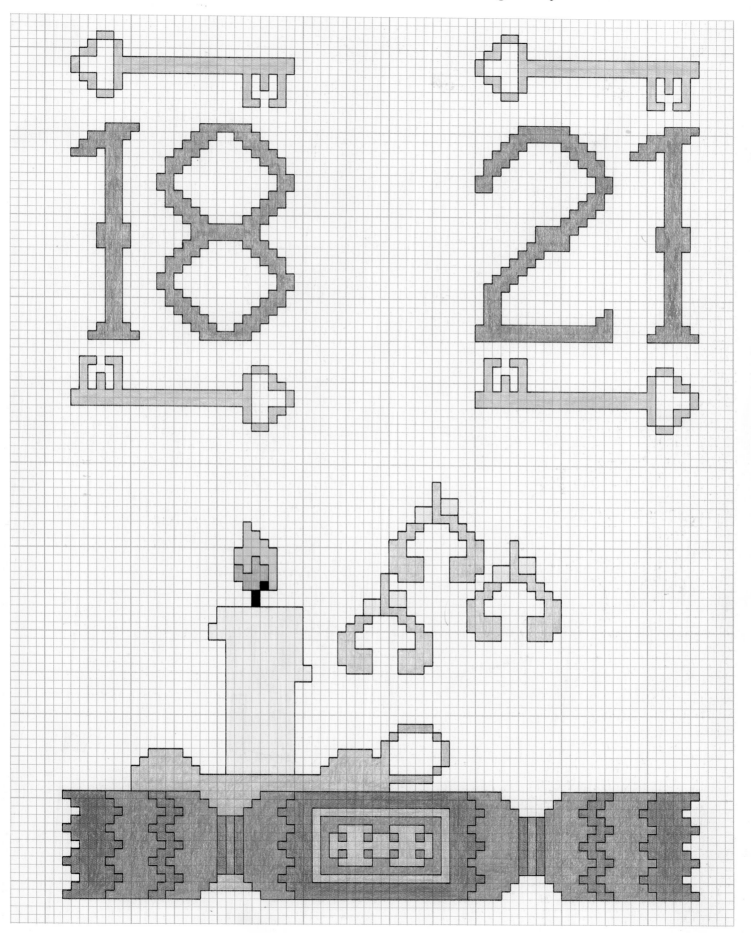

Porcelain trinket boxes

These beautiful trinket boxes illustrating the signs of the Zodiac make ideal gifts as they are both useful and decorative – an ideal birthday present or a thank-you gift for someone special. They can adorn a dressing table, small table or even a mantelpiece.

Capricorn	22 December–20 January
Aquarius	21 January–19 February
Pisces	20 February–20 March
Aries	21 March–20 April
Taurus	21 April–21 May
Gemini	22 May–21 June
Cancer	22 June–23 July
Leo	24 July–23 August
Virgo	24 August–23 September
Libra	24 September–23 October
Scorpio	24 October–22 November
Sagittarius	23 November–21 December

Materials

Framecraft round porcelain trinket boxes with 6.5 cm (2 ⅝") diameter lids
White Aida measuring 13 cm (5") square, 18 stitches to the inch (per trinket box)
DMC six-strand stranded embroidery cotton
Tapestry needle (No. 26)

Instructions

1   Work the cross stitch embroideries centrally onto the Aida, using two strands of stranded cotton throughout.

2   Once complete, press the work.

3   Place the finished cross stitch embroidery face up on a firm, flat surface.

4   Gently remove all parts from the trinket box lid, using the rim of the lid to centre the design.

5   Once the design is centred, draw around the outer edge onto the fabric. Remove the lid and cut the fabric to size.

6   To assemble the lid, replace the clear acetate and place your design centrally into the lid, with the right side to the acetate. Place the sponge behind your design. Push the metal locking disc very firmly into place using thumb pressure, with the raised side of the disc facing the sponge. When the locking disc is tightly in position, use a little glue to secure the flock lining-card to it.

Halloween picture

What better way is there to display your handiwork for all to admire than to give it a prominent position on the wall of your favourite room? I have designed an idea for Halloween and for the birth of a new baby.

Materials

Halloween picture measuring 29 x 25.5 cm (11 ½ x 10") unframed:
White Aida measuring 34.5 x 30.5 cm (13 ½ x 12"), 14 stitches to the inch
Mounting board 29 x 25.5 cm (11 ½ x 10")
Masking tape
DMC six-strand stranded embroidery cotton
Tapestry needles (No. 24 and No. 26)
Picture frame of your choice

Instructions

1 Complete the embroidery centrally on your cross stitch fabric, using two strands of stranded cotton for the cross stitch and one strand for the backstitch.

Mounting your embroidery

1 Press your completed cross stitch so that it is nice and flat.

2 To mount your embroidery you will need to stretch it over the mounting board. Place the embroidery face down on to a clean, flat surface and put the mounting board centrally onto it. Remember to cut your mounting board 2.5–4 cm (1–1 ½") smaller than your needlework fabric.

3 Fold one edge of the fabric over the mounting board (ensuring that it is perfectly straight) and secure with pins.

4 Secure the opposite edge in the same way, making sure that the fabric is straight and taut.

5 Use masking tape to secure the edges of the fabric onto the back of the mounting board and then remove the pins.

6 Repeat this procedure on the remaining two edges.

Tip See page 69 for two illustrations which will be helpful when mounting your embroidery.

Baby picture

Materials

Birth of a baby picture measuring
28 x 25 cm (11 x 10") unframed:
Navy Aida measuring 33 x 30.5 cm
(13 x 12"), 18 stitches to the inch
Mounting board 28 x 25 cm (11 x 10")
Masking tape
DMC six-strand stranded embroidery cotton
Tapestry needles (No. 24 and No. 26)
Picture frame of your choice

Instructions

1   Complete the embroidery centrally on your
cross stitch fabric, using two strands of
stranded cotton for the cross stitch and one
strand for the backstitch.

2   To mount your embroidery, follow the
instructions for the Halloween picture.

3   Your embroidery picture is now ready to be
framed. The best result will be achieved by a
professional framer. If you want glass in your
frame, it is better to use non-reflective glass.
It is well worth the extra expense.

Tip If you find the procedure for mounting the
embroidery too fiddly, try a self-stick mounting
board from Press-On Products Inc. These are
available in five different sizes from department
stores and craft shops. They really are a treat to
work with and make the job very easy. You
simply cut the board to size as before, peel off
the backing and lay your needlework fabric onto
the board, making sure it is centred. When you
are satisfied, press down very hard over the
entire needlework surface, then tape the
excess fabric to the back of the mounting
board with masking tape.

46 acc
69 dow

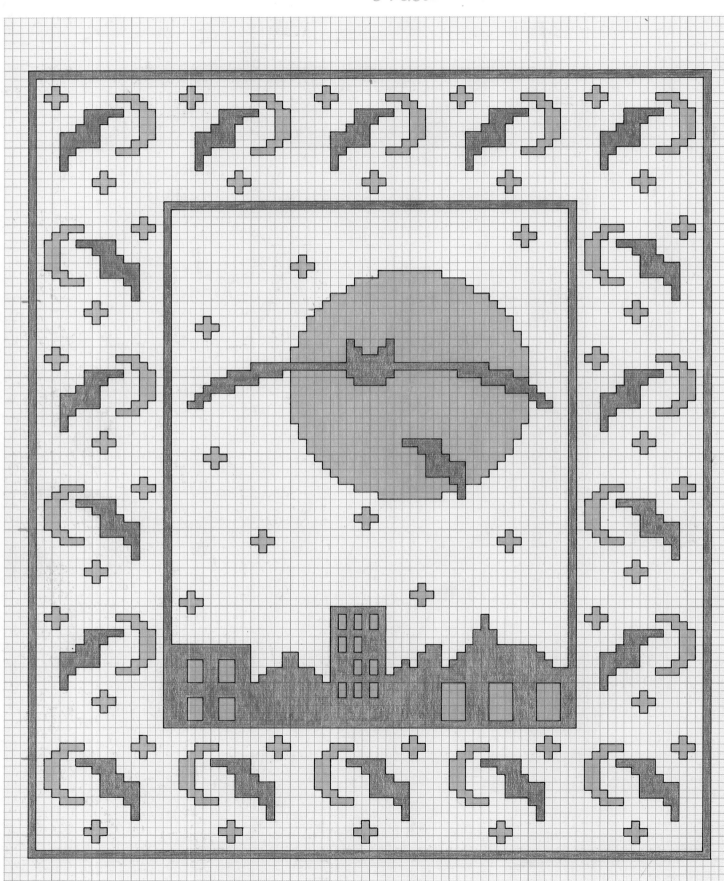

52 acc
56 dow

chapter three

Designs for Children

In this chapter, I have chosen designs which will appeal to children of all ages and have made the projects both decorative and practical. There is a selection of borders and motifs to embroider onto children's clothes using waste canvas, a cot cover with cute teddy bear designs, a toy box and framed picture with more teddy bears, children's alphabets and draw-string bags featuring horses and dinosaurs which can be used as tote bags or shoe bags. You could personalize the projects using the decorative alphabet. Or why not make a set of framed pictures to match the cot cover, using the teddy designs on pages 44–45?

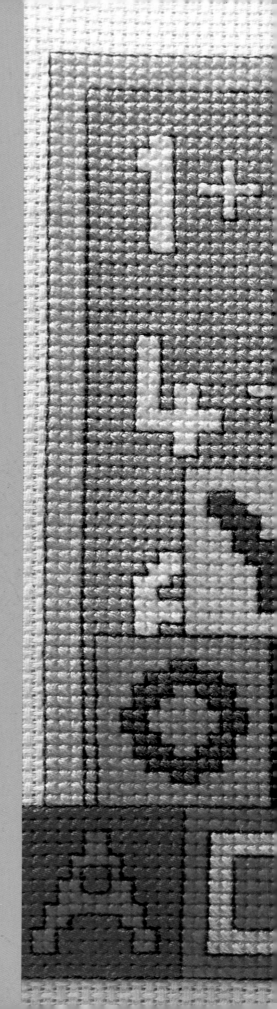

Panels and borders for clothes

Decorate your children's clothes with these lovely designs using waste canvas. It is so easy and the results are very satisfying.

Materials

Waste canvas, 14 stitches to the inch
Tacking thread
DMC six-strand stranded embroidery cotton
Tapestry needle (No. 24)
Pair of fine tweezers
Spray bottle of water

Instructions

In order to calculate the amount of waste canvas required, estimate the finished size of your chosen design and cut the canvas about two inches larger all round.

Dog design: approximately 15 x 12.5 cm (6 x 5") of waste canvas
Rabbit and carrot design: approximately 13 cm (5") deep and your chosen border width

1   To ensure that your finished embroidery is straight, align the blue threads either horizontally or vertically with the weave of the fabric or the seams of the garment.

2   Pin the canvas centrally over the area where the design is to be stitched and tack the waste canvas in place around the edges. Once this is done, remove the pins.

3   Stitch the design as you would any other evenweave fabric, treating each pair of canvas threads as a single thread. Start stitching at the top of the design and work downwards (using two strands for the cross stitch and one for the backstitch). Start and finish threads as before – anchor your first few stitches and thread the ends in on the back of the work when finishing off. If the garments are going to be washed frequently, you may want to begin and end threads with a small knot for added security.

4   When you have completed the embroidery, cut away the extra canvas leaving approximately 1 cm (½") around the design. Dampen the right side with slightly warm water (do not soak it) and leave it for few minutes until the sizing softens. Use the tweezers to pull out each of the canvas threads one at a time. Resist the temptation to pull out more than one thread at a time as you risk damaging the embroidery. Moisten again if required. As if by magic, you are now left with the finished design on your garment.

5   Place your embroidered garment wrong-side up over a dry towel and press, taking care not to flatten the stitches. If you use fabric which is dry clean only, the canvas threads can be softened by rubbing them together (taking care not to damage the embroidery). You should then be able to remove the threads one by one without having to use water.

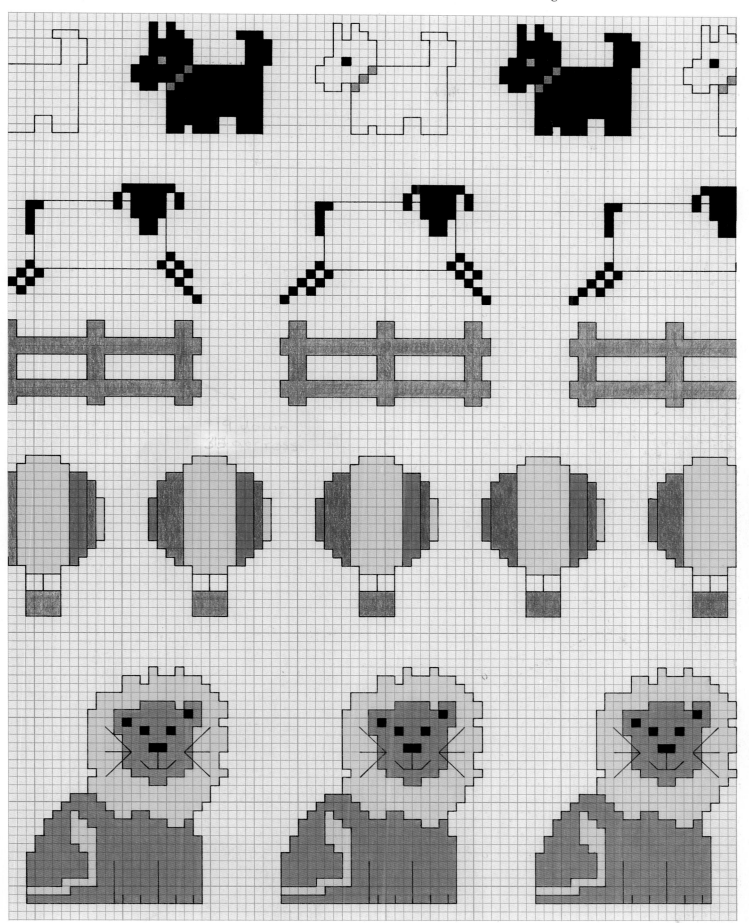

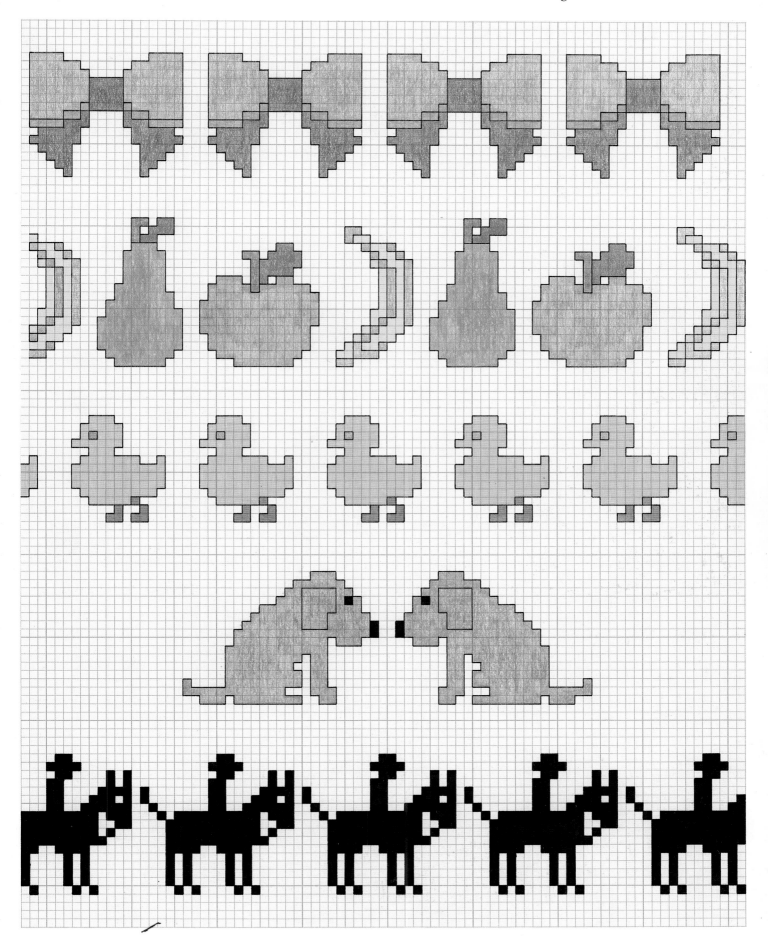

Teddy bear cot cover

This wonderful Anne fabric, produced in
13 cm (5") squares separated by double
tramlines, is ideal for a cot cover. Who could
possibly resist these playful teddies?

Materials

Anne fabric measuring 58.5 x 71 cm
(23 x 28")
DMC six-strand stranded embroidery cotton
Tapestry needle (No. 26)
Sewing thread to match fabric

Instructions

1   Follow the diagram to cut your fabric to size.
    Use a sewing machine to zig-zag around
    the border.

2   Work each teddy centrally on the designated
    squares (see diagram), using two strands of
    stranded cotton for the cross stitch and one
    strand for the backstitch.

3   Once you have finished, trim the fabric to the
    final size and fray out the edges. Remove the
    fabric strands one at a time until you reach
    the zig-zag stitch line. Brush with a stiff brush.

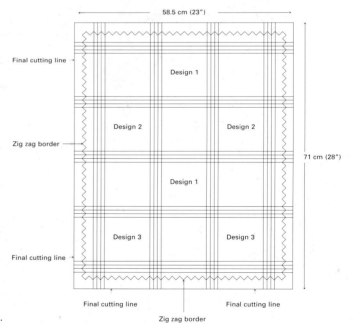

Designs for Children

Design 1

Design 2

46 accross
70 down

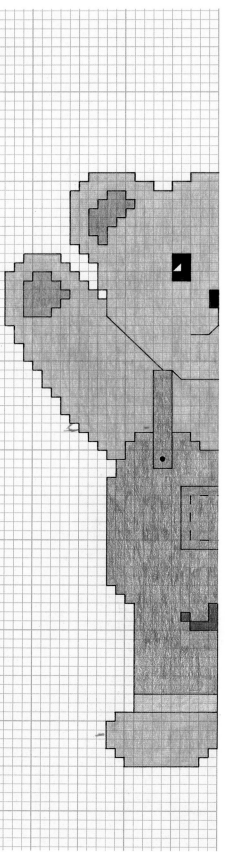

Design 3

Toy box

This toy box is made from a sewing box, part of a beautiful range of self-upholster furniture available from craft suppliers and department stores. The box is designed to take a design measuring 30.5 x 38 cm (12 x 15").

Materials

White Aida and calico measuring 45 x 53 cm (17 ¾ x 20"), 14 stitches to the inch
DMC six-strand stranded embroidery cotton
Self-cover sewing box
Tapestry needle (No. 24)

Instructions

1 Complete your embroidery using two strands of the DMC stranded cotton for the cross stitch and one strand for the backstitch.

2 Now you can assemble the toy box. As the fit between the top of the box and its frame is designed to accommodate a thicker piece of needlepoint, cover the top with calico first.

3 Remove the top of the toy box by undoing the screws which are recessed into the under frame. Put them aside.

4 Lay the toy box top on a flat surface, pad uppermost. Measure the length from the surface, over and down to the other surface. Do this in both dimensions. Add three inches to each dimension to obtain the material size.

Fitting the material

1 Turn over ¼" of raw edge all round and tack in place.

2 Lay the material, right-side down, on a flat surface. Lay the box top, pad down, on the material so that an equal amount of material shows all around the top.

3 Squeeze the pad down onto the material along one of the long edges, by kneeling on it. Bring the material over the edge and tack it down with ¼" tacks through the stitched double layer. Work outwards, bringing the material over the edge as you go along. Keep the material edge straight and equidistant from the edge of the top, tacking it down about every 1 ½". Work both corners. The material can be fixed using a staple gun or by lacing with fine twine or strong thread.

4 Squeeze the box top down along the opposite edge and repeat the tacking process as above.

5 Repeat the process along one of the remaining edges. This time, fold the material at the corners, and pull the folds inwards to prevent any bulging. Repeat the process on the last edge. For a neater finish, sew or glue a piece of calico or similar material to the underside of the pad before replacing it on the box.

6 Replace the top on the sewing box, gently pressing it into the corners where the fit will be the tightest. Rescrew the top to the frame.

Winter teddies picture

The 'Winter teddies' framed picture would make an ideal Christmas present, and is sure to delight any child!

Materials

Picture measuring 33 x 26.5 cm
(13 x 10 ½") unframed:
White Aida measuring 38 x 32 cm
(15 x 12 ½"), 14 stitches to the inch
Mounting board measuring 33 x 26.5 cm
(13 x 10 ½")
Masking tape
DMC six-strand stranded embroidery cotton
Tapestry needle (No. 24)
Picture frame of your choice

Instructions

1 Complete the embroidery centrally on your cross stitch fabric, using two strands of stranded cotton for the cross stitch and one strand for the backstitch.

2 To mount and frame your embroidery, follow the instructions given for the framed pictures on pages 28–29.

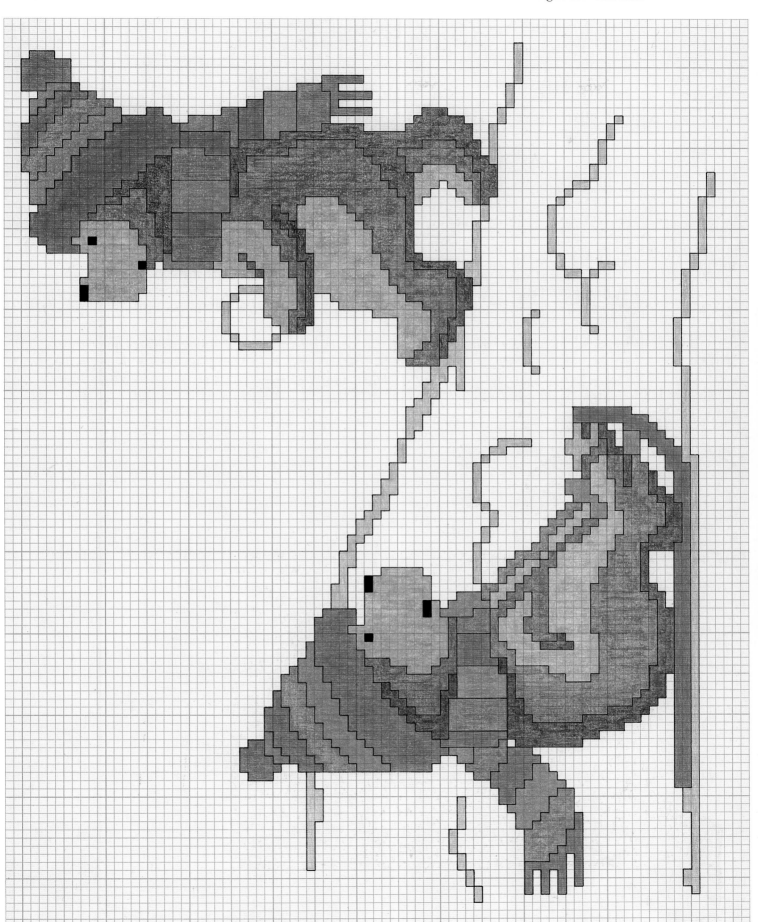

106 accross

43 down

Children's alphabets

A hand-embroidered name or initial provides the perfect finishing touch for many gifts.

Materials

Key ring: Framecraft round key ring measuring 1 ½" (4 cm) in diameter
Small scrap of fabric, 20 stitches to the inch
DMC six-strand stranded cotton
Tapestry needle (No. 26)

Miniature brass frame: Framecraft miniature brass frame measuring 2 ⅞ x 2" (7.5 x 5 cm)
White Aida measuring 4 x 5" (10 x 13 cm),
14 stitches to the inch
DMC six-strand stranded cotton
Tapestry needle (No. 24)

Trinket box: Framecraft round porcelain trinket box measuring 1 ¼" (32 mm)
Small scrap of fabric, 20 stitches to the inch
DMC six-strand stranded cotton (use 1 strand)
Tapestry needle (No. 26)

Greetings card: DMC presentation card in red with a rectangular cut-out
White Aida measuring 4 ½ x 3 ½" (12 x 9 cm),
14 stitches to the inch
DMC six-strand stranded cotton
Tapestry needle (No. 24)

Instructions

Key ring:

1   Work the design centrally on the fabric using one strand throughout. Press if required.

2   Place the embroidery face-up on a flat surface. Gently remove the backing disc from the key ring, using it to centre the design.

3   Draw around the outer edge onto the fabric, remove the disc and cut the fabric to size.

4   To assemble the key ring, place your design face-down into the recess on the back of the key ring, and push the clear plastic backing disc firmly into place using thumb pressure.

Miniature brass frame:

1   Work the cross stitch embroidery centrally onto the Aida using two strands of stranded cotton, and one strand for the backstitch outlines. Press if required.

2   Place the embroidery face-up on a firm, flat surface. Gently remove all parts of the frame, using the template provided to draw around your design, ensuring it is central.

3   To assemble the frame, place the clear acetate into the frame, followed by your embroidery, then the thin card, and finally the backing.

Trinket box:

1   Refer to page 24 for making-up instructions.

Greetings card:

1   Refer to page 18 for making-up instructions.

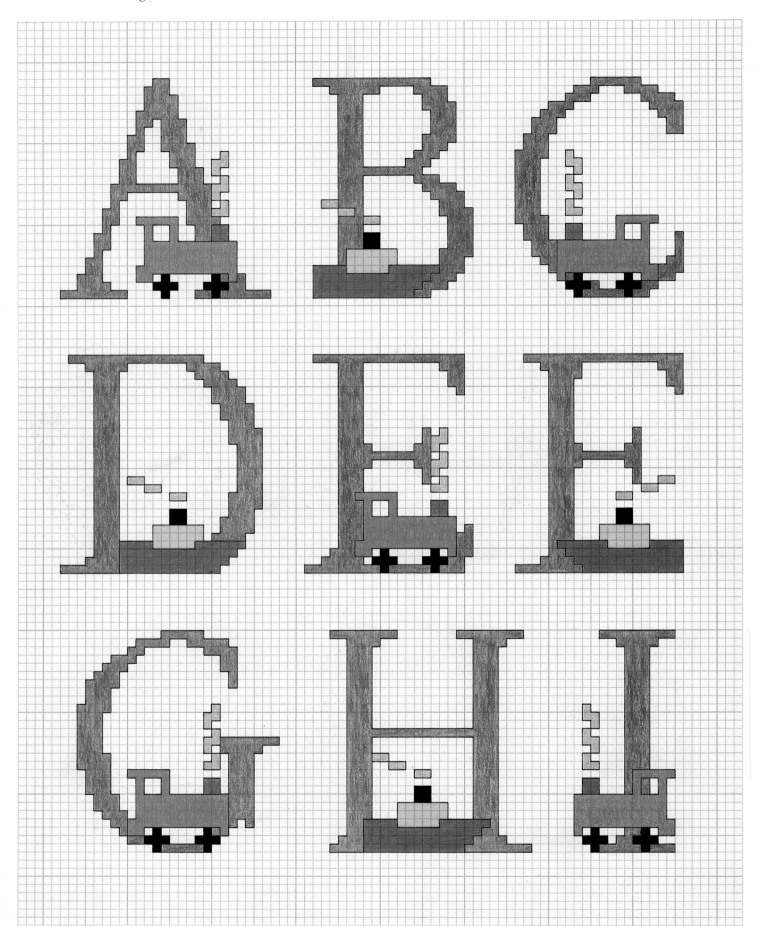

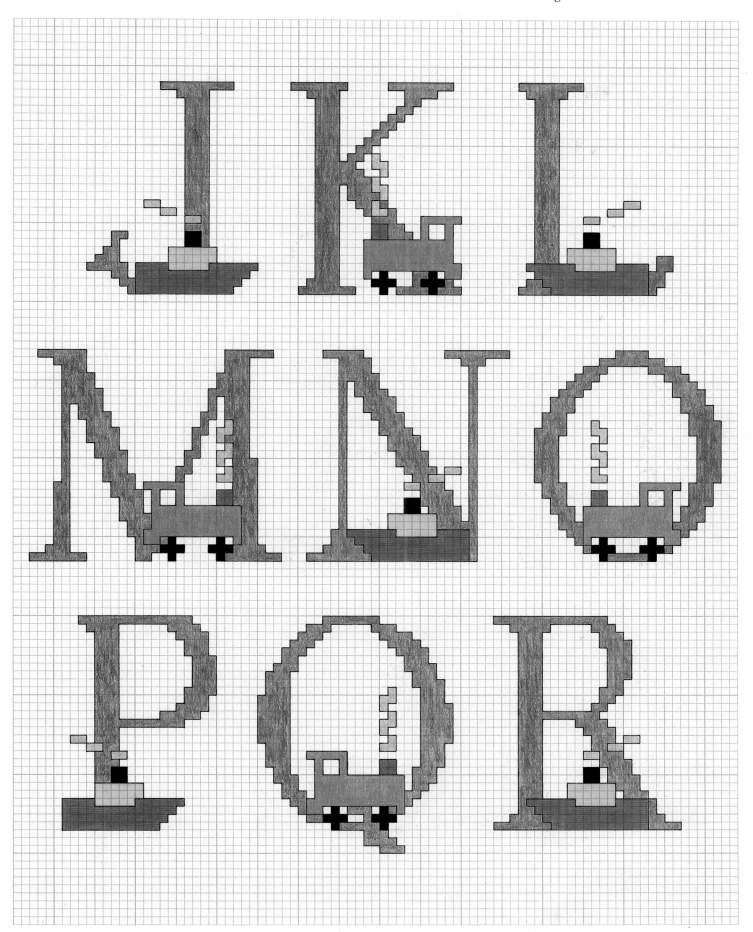

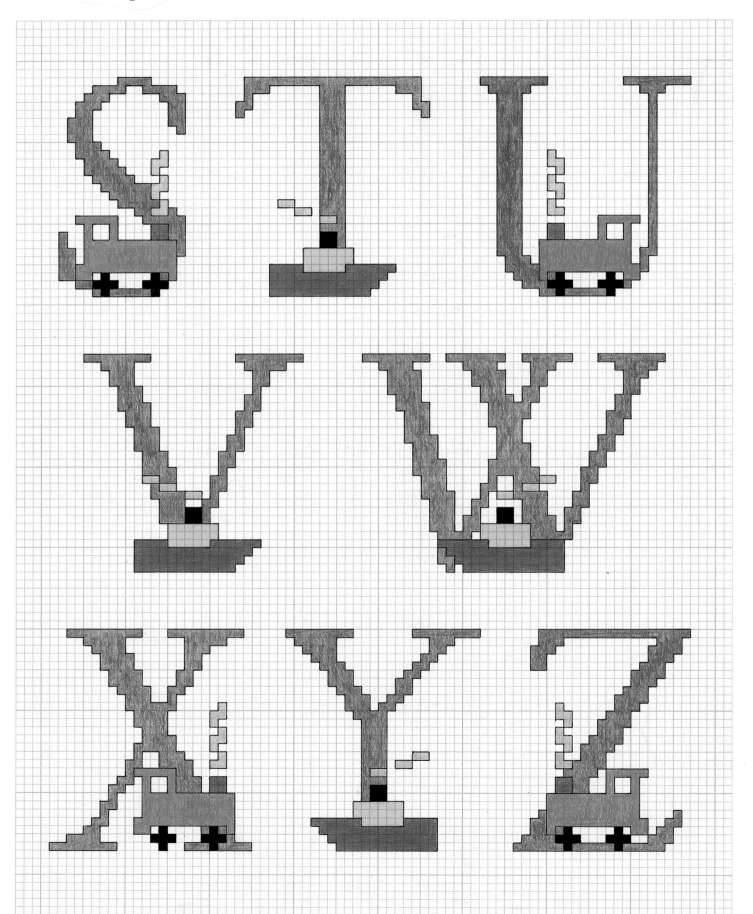

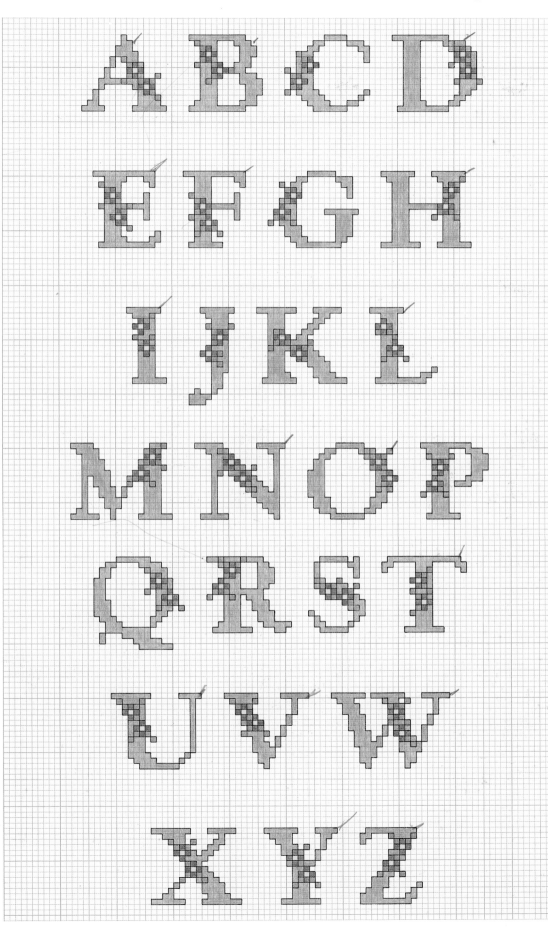

21 x 15

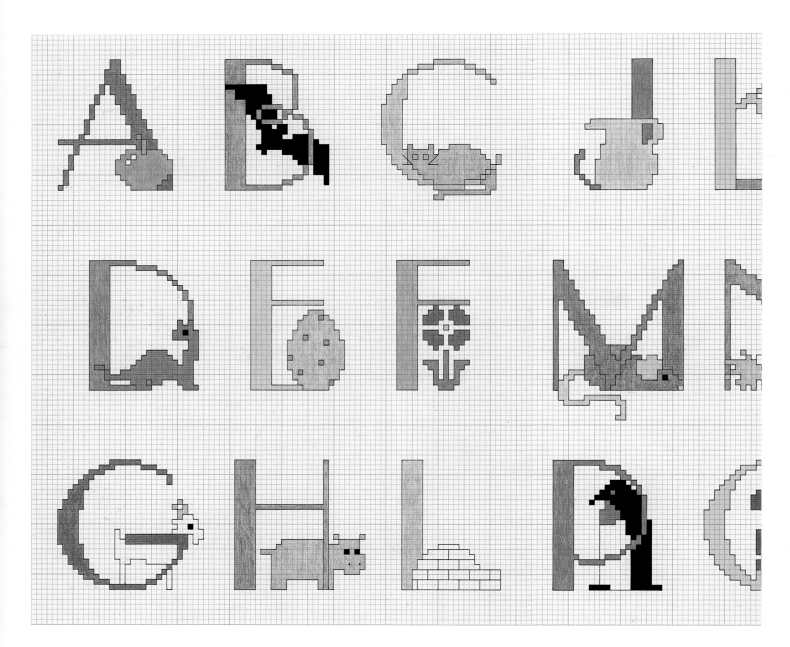

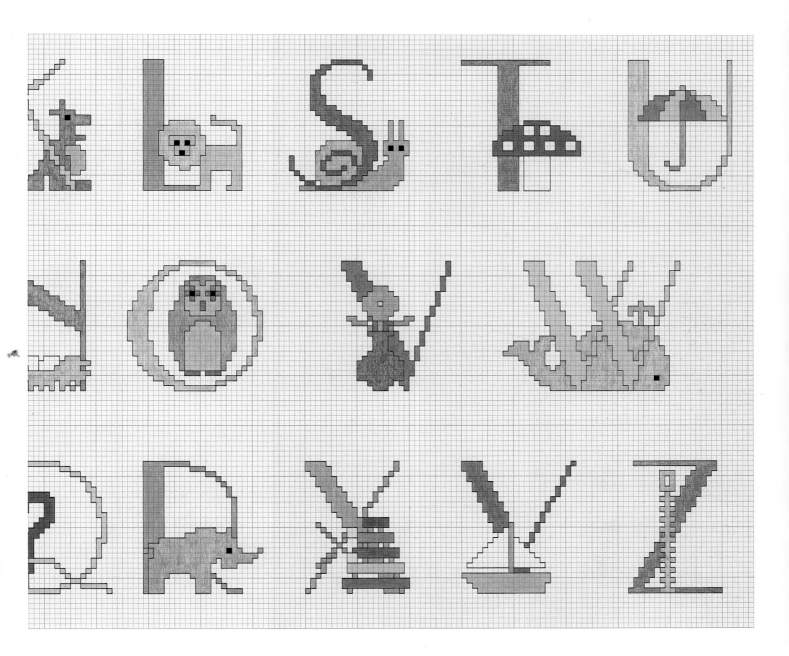

Dinosaur shoe bag and horse tote bag

These useful bags make extremely practical gifts. They will be a bright and attractive feature in the playroom or at school or nursery, and are suitable for children of any age group. The bags have a drawstring top and are large enough and strong enough to hold a pair of children's plimsolls, or many small toys.

Materials

Each bag:
White cord 1.5 m (59") long and 6 mm (¼") wide
White Hardanger, 2 pieces measuring approximately 33 x 45 cm (13 x 17 ½"), 22 stitches to the inch
White cotton fabric, 2 pieces measuring 33 x 45 cm (13 x 17 ½") for the lining
DMC six-strand stranded embroidery cotton
Tapestry needle (No. 26)
Sewing thread to match fabric

Instructions

1 Complete the picture for the front of the bag using three strands of stranded cotton for the cross stitch and two strands for the backstitch, sewing over two threads of the Hardanger so that in effect there are 11 stitches to the inch. Ensure that a clearance is left around the finished embroidery of 6.5 cm (2 ½") at the sides and bottom, and 14 cm (5 ½") at the top. These measurements include a 1.5 cm (½") seam allowance.

2 Place the two pieces of Hardanger right-sides together. Stitch the side seams down from the top for 4 cm (1 ½"). Leave a gap of 2.5 cm (1"), then recommence stitching the side seams to the bottom (Fig. 1).

3 Press the side seams open around the gap, and then top stitch 6 mm (¼") from the edge (Fig. 2).

4 Stitch the bottom seam and clip the corners.

5 Turn to the right side and press.

6 Place the two pieces of lining fabric right-sides together and stitch the side seams. Stitch the bottom seam, leaving an opening of 15 cm (6") at the centre (Fig. 3). Clip the corners.

7 Place the outer bag into the lining, right sides together. Stitch around the top edge.

8 Turn right side out, easing through the opening at the bottom of the lining. Slip stitch the lining together at the bottom.

9 Press the top edge of the bag along the seam.

10 Top stitch around the bag 6 mm (¼") above the cord opening and again below (Fig. 4).

11 Take the cord and thread it twice round through the casement made by the two rows of stitches. Join the ends together, and draw out a loop of cord at each side.

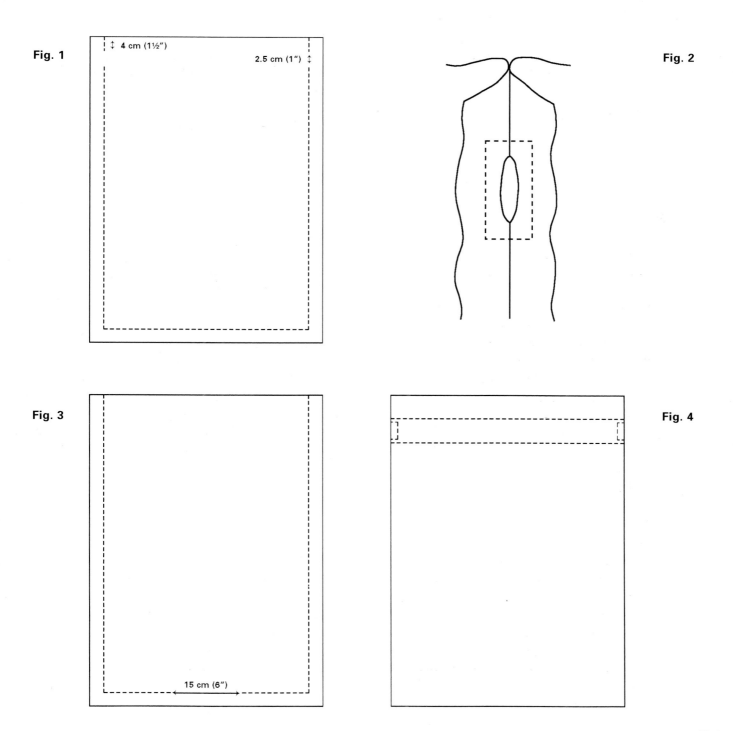

Fig. 1

↕ 4 cm (1½")

2.5 cm (1") ↕

Fig. 2

Fig. 3

15 cm (6")

Fig. 4

446 acc
49 down

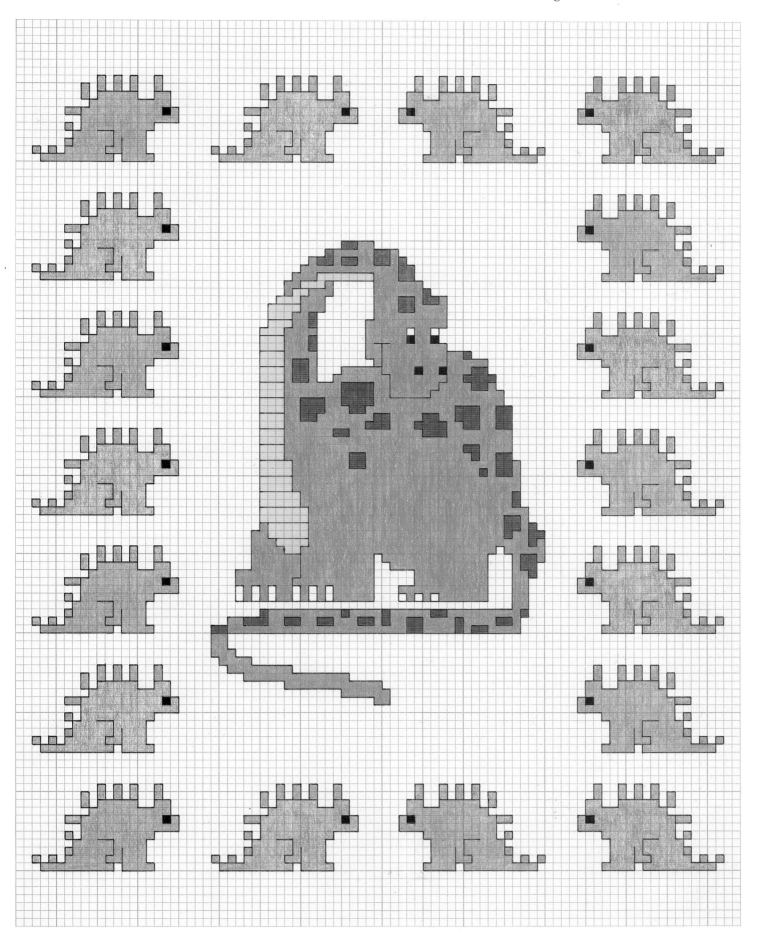

chapter four

Designs for the Home

This chapter contains a delightful assortment of designs and projects for use in any room. There is a unique teapot sampler for the kitchen, all-over repeat patterns for trays and cushions, rows of borders for table linen and footstools and sun-and-moon dressing table mats for the bedroom. Add a personal touch to your home by creating soft furnishings embellished with these designs. Why not make some curtain tie-backs to match the cushions?

Teapot sampler

This delightful teapot sampler is designed to complement a traditional kitchen with a pine dresser and lovely blue-and-white ceramics. If you have a modern kitchen, simply change the colour of the teapots to match your personal decor, whether it is red and white or pink and grey, and have the sampler framed in a modern co-ordinating frame to complete the effect.

Materials

Sampler measuring 43.5 x 30.5 cm
(17 x 12") unframed:
White Aida measuring 48.5 x 35.5 cm
(19 x 14"), 14 stitches to the inch
Mounting board 43.5 x 30.5 cm (17 x 12")
Masking tape
DMC six-strand stranded embroidery cotton
Tapestry needle (No. 24)
Picture frame of your choice

Instructions

1 Complete the embroidery centrally on your cross stitch fabric, using two strands of stranded cotton for the cross stitch and one for the backstitch.

Mounting your embroidery

1 Press your completed cross stitch so that it is nice and flat.

2 To mount your embroidery you will need to stretch it over the mounting board. Place the embroidery face down on to a clean, flat surface and put the mounting board centrally onto it. Remember to cut your mounting board 2.5–4 cm (1–1 ½") smaller than your needlework fabric.

3 Mitre the corners and fold the fabric over to the back of the mounting board. Ensure that it is perfectly straight and secure with pins (Fig. 1).

4 Secure the opposite edge in the same way, making sure that the fabric is straight and taut.

5 Use masking tape to secure the edges of the fabric onto the back of the mounting board and then remove the pins (Fig. 2).

6 Repeat this procedure on the remaining two edges.

Tip It is preferable to have your picture framed by a professional and as I have mentioned before, non-reflective glass is well worth the extra expense.

Fig. 1

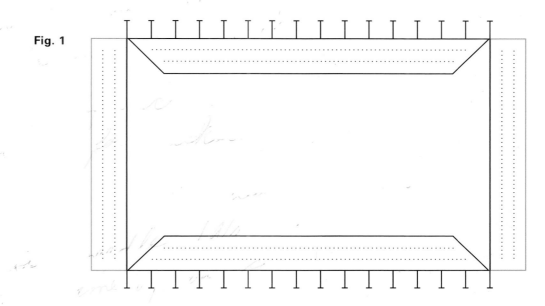

Fig. 2

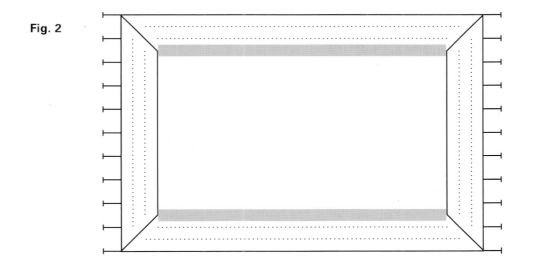

167 accross
105 down

Tea-time tray

When friends call in for tea, impress them with this beautiful tray, lovingly embroidered and mounted under glass. The tartan repeat pattern is on page 77.

Materials

Tray measuring 24 cm (9 ½") square:
White Aida measuring 28 cm (11") square,
14 stitches to the inch
DMC six-strand stranded embroidery thread
Tapestry needle (No. 24)
Masking tape
Framecraft square wooden tray

Instructions

1   Complete the embroidery centrally on the Aida using two strands of the stranded embroidery cotton throughout. Press the finished embroidery if required. .

2   Place the embroidery face down on a clean, flat surface. Take the thick card provided with the tray and place it exactly in the centre of the embroidery.

3   Fold the edges of the excess fabric over the card, working one side and then the opposite side, and secure both with masking tape.

4   When you are sure the design is centred, secure the corners firmly.

5   Insert the mounted embroidery into the tray, following the manufacturer's instructions.

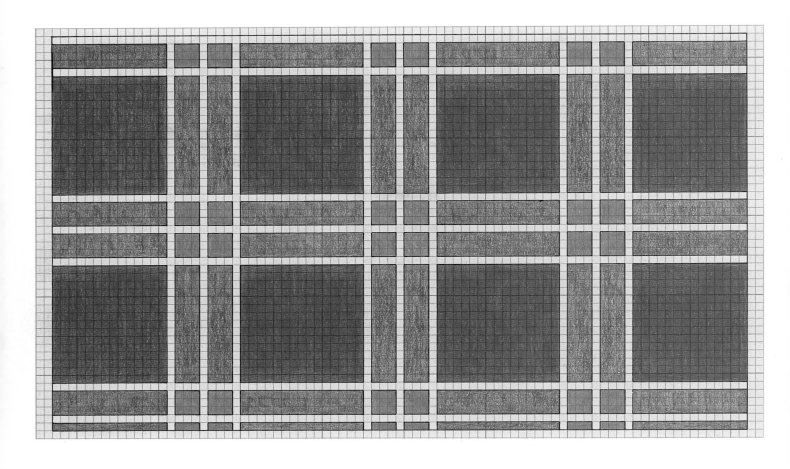

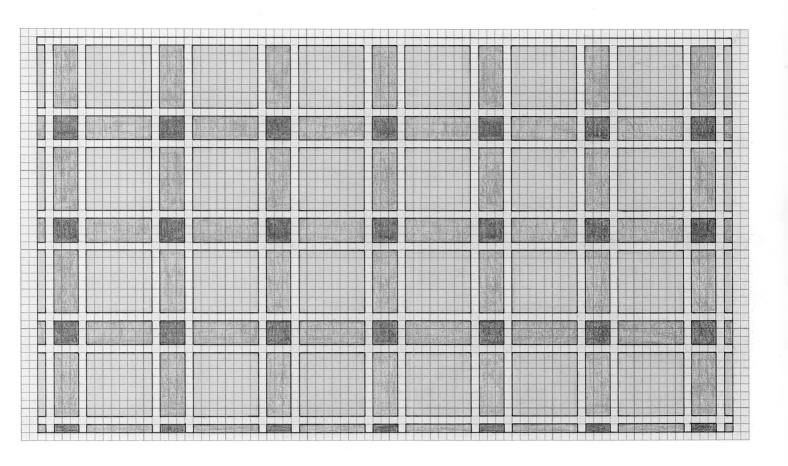

Table linen and hand towel

By adapting the decorative borders on pages 80–83, you can create these striking napkins and placemats to brighten up any dinner table. After washing the dishes, dry your hands on this pretty hand towel, decorated with the ice-cream sundaes design on page 81. The napkins, placemats and hand towel featured are worked on 28-count Quaker cloth.

Materials

Piece of Quaker cloth measuring 33 x 48 cm (13 x 19") for each placemat
Piece of Quaker cloth measuring 40.5 x 40.5 cm (16 x 16") for each dinner napkin
Piece of Quaker cloth measuring 63.5 x 38 cm (25 x 15") for the hand towel
DMC six-strand stranded embroidery cotton
Tapestry needle (No. 26)

Instructions

1 Complete the embroidery on the linen in the position you think best, using two strands of the stranded cotton and sewing over two threads of the fabric, in effect making it 14-count.

2 Press if required.

3 Finish off the edges either by fraying or by sewing a double hem.

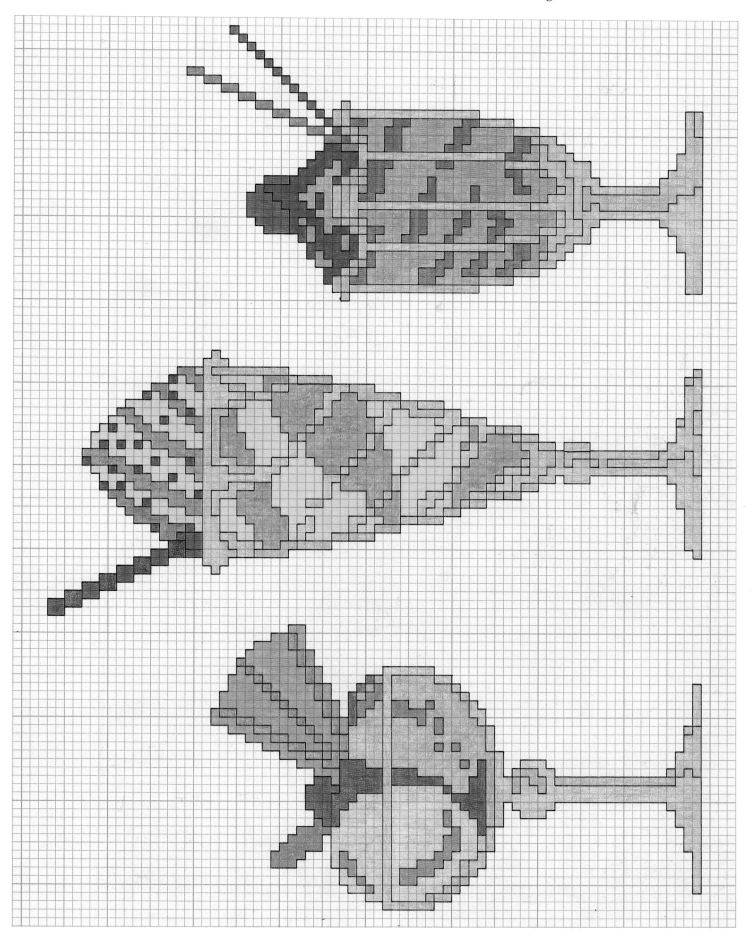

Motif cushions

These striking cushions feature the heraldic repeat patterns on pages 86–87. They are simple to make and will be a focal point of any room, whether you scatter them over a bed or a favourite chair.

Materials

Cushion measuring 35.5 cm (14") square:
White Aida square measuring 38 cm (15"),
14 stitches to the inch
Contrasting fabric, e.g. Aida, of the same size to back your cushion
Square cushion pad 35.5 cm (14")
Tapestry needle (No. 24)
Sewing thread to match fabric
(Measurements include a 1.5 cm (½") seam allowance)

Instructions

1   Complete the embroidery centrally on the Aida, using two strands of stranded cotton throughout. When you have completed the design, press if required.

2   Take your backing material and place it onto the Aida, right-sides facing. Pin and tack three sides together.

3   Machine stitch around these three sides. Remove pins and tacking stitches. Turn to the right side.

4   Press in the seam allowance on the open edge, place the cushion pad inside the cover and hand oversew the open edge closed.

5   If you prefer a more decorative finish, you could buy some cord or piping from your local department store to stitch around the edges when your cushion is complete. You could also add matching tassels to each corner for a really elaborate look!

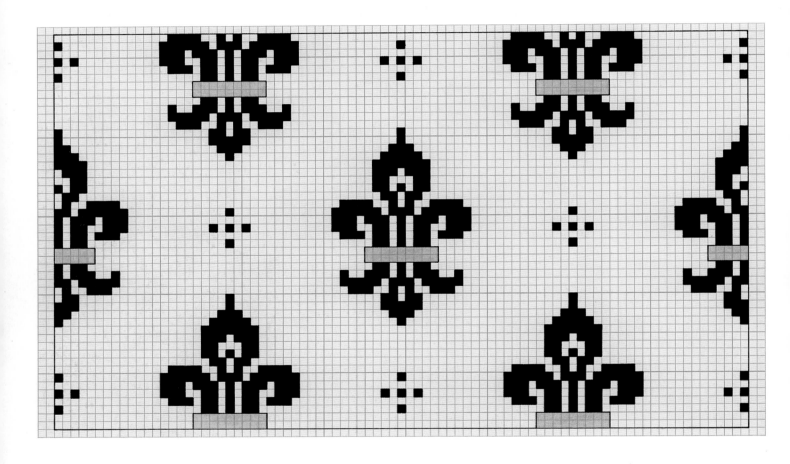

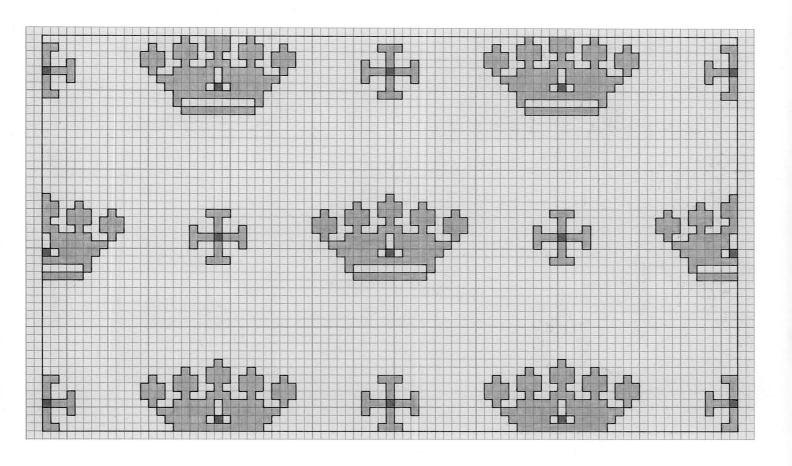

Sun-and-moon dressing table mats

This enchanting dressing table set features adaptations of the sun-and-moon designs on pages 90–91.

The runner features the sun and two repeats of the sun-and-moon borders, whilst the mats depict the stars and moon centrally, surrounded by the sun-and-moon border.

Materials

Silver fleck Bellana measuring 73 x 32 cm
(28 ¾ x 12 ⅝"), 20 stitches to the inch
for the runner
Silver fleck Bellana, 2 x 32 cm (12 ⅝") squares,
20 stitches to the inch for the mats
DMC six-strand stranded embroidery cotton
Tapestry needle (No. 26)

Instructions

1   Complete the main motifs centrally on the Bellana pieces, followed by the border designs, at a distance of 8 cm (3") from the edge of the fabric, using one strand of cotton throughout. Press if required.

2   To make a decorative edge, fray out the edges of the fabric for 2.5 cm (1"). Do this by very carefully removing the threads of the fabric one at a time.

64 down.
37 acc ...

64 accross
64 down

Conversion Chart

Shade name	DMC	Anchor	Coats	Madeira
White	White	2	1001	White
Very Dark Lavender	208	110	4301	0804
Medium Lavender	210	104	4303	0802
Medium Mahogany Brown	301	349		2306
Lemon Yellow	307	289	2290	0104
Deep Rose Red	309	42	3284	0507
Black	310	403	8403	Black
Medium Navy Blue	311	148		1006
Light Navy Blue	312	147	7979	1005
Medium Steel Grey	317	400	8512	1714
Christmas Red	321	47	3500	0510
Dark Baby Blue	322	978	7978	1004
Medium Baby Blue	334	161	7977	1003
Dark Pink	335	42	3283	0506
Red	349	13	2335	0212
Dark Peach	351	10	3012	0214
Dark Mahogany Brown	400			
Very Dark Steel Grey	413	401	8514	1713
Pale Grey	415	398	8510	1803
Medium Brown	433	371	5471	2008
Light Brown	434	309	5000	2009
Very Light Brown	435	365	5371	2010
Tan Brown	436	363	5943	2011
Dark Christmas Red	498	47		0511
Very Dark Violet	550	101	4108	0714
Medium Violet	553	98	4097	0712
Bright Orange Red	606	335	2334	0209
Very Dark Drab Brown	610	906		2106
Drab Brown	612	832		2108
Dark Beaver Grey	645	400	8500	1811
Bright Christmas Red	666	46	3046	0210
Light Old Gold	676	891	2305	2208
Very Light Old Gold	677	886	2300	2207
Dark Old Gold	680	901	5374	2210

Shade name	DMC	Anchor	Coats	Madeira
Dark Kelly Green	701	227	6226	1305
Kelly Green	702	226	6239	1306
Topaz Yellow	725	306	2298	0108
Very Light Topaz Yellow	727	293		0110
Medium Old Gold	729			
Very Light Tan	738	942	5375	2013
Tangerine Orange	740	316	2099	0202
Medium Tangerine Orange	741	304	2314	0201
Dark Yellow	743	297	2302	0113
Light Pearl Grey	762	397	8510	1804
Very Dark Topaz Brown	780	309		2214
Dark Topaz Brown	781	308		2213
Medium Topaz Brown	782	307		2212
Christmas Gold	783	307		2211
Royal Blue	797	132	7023	0912
Medium Delft Blue	799	130	7030	0910
Dark Coffee Brown	801	357	5475	2007
Delft Blue	809	130	7021	0909
Medium Garnet Red	815	43	3000	0513
Garnet Red	816	20	3410	0512
Dark Navy Blue	823	150		1008
Dark Blue	825	162		1011
Medium Blue	826	161		1012
Light Golden Wheat Yellow	834	874		2204
Very Dark Beaver Grey	844	401		1810
Dark Carnation Red	891	29		0411
Very Dark Coffee Brown	898	360	5476	2006
Medium Pink	899	27	3282	0505
Dark Emerald Green	910	228	6031	1301
Light Emerald Green	912	209	6225	1212
Dark Dusty Rose Pink	961	40		0610
Very Light Dusty Rose Pink	963	48		0608
Light Pumpkin Orange	970	316	2327	0204
Deep Canary Yellow	972	303		0107

Shade name	DMC	Anchor	Coats	Madeira
Bright Canary Yellow	973	297		0105
Medium Golden Brown	976	309		2302
Dark Forest Green	987	245	6258	1403
Light Forest Green	989	256	6266	1401
Aquamarine	992	187	6186	1202
Medium Electric Blue	996	433	7001	1103
Very Dark Brown Grey	3021	382	5395	1904
Brown Grey	3022	8581		1903
Medium Beige	3032			
Pale Golden Wheat	3047	886	2300	2205
Very Light Golden Yellow	3078	292	2292	0102
Baby Blue	3325	159	7976	1002
Pink	3326	26	3126	0504

List of Suppliers

UK

DMC Creative World Ltd
Pullman Road
Wigston
Leicester LE8 2DY

Framecraft Miniatures Ltd
372-376 Summer Lane
Hockley
Birmingham B19 3QA

H W Peel & Company Ltd
Norwester House
Fairway Drive
Greenford
Middlesex UB6 8PW

Woodhouse
Rock Channel
Rye
East Sussex TN31 7HJ

Mary Allen
Wirksworth
Derbyshire DE4 4BN

Needlecraft Needs
11 Leigh Road
Wimborne
Dorset BH21 1AB

Barnyarns
Old Pitts Farm
Langrish
Petersfield
Hampshire GU32 1RG

Madeira Threads (UK) Ltd
Thirsk Industrial Park
York Road
Thirsk
North Yorkshire YO7 3BX

Campden Needlecraft Centre
High Street
Chipping Campden
Gloucestershire GL55 6AG

De Havilland Embroidery
27 Old Gloucester Street
London WC1 3XX

John Lewis & Co
278-306 Oxford Street
London W1A 1EX

Maple Textiles
188-90 Maple Road
Penge
London SE20 8HT

Threadbare
Glenfield Park
Glenfield Road
Nelson
Lancs BB9 8AR

Whaleys (Bradford) Ltd
Harris Court
Great Horton
Bradford
West Yorkshire BD7 4EQ

The Embroidery Shop
51 William Street
Edinburgh EH3 7LW

Anchor and Coats
Coats Leisure Crafts Group
39 Durham Street
Glasgow G41 1BS

Christine Riley
53 Barclay Street
Stonehaven
Kincardineshire AB3 2AR

Australia

Clifton H Joseph & Son Pty Ltd
391-393 Little Lonsdale Street
Melbourne
Victoria 3000

Altamira
34 Murphy Street
South Yarra
Melbourne
Victoria 3141

Tapestry Rose
PO Box 366
Canterbury
Victoria 3126

Coats Patons Crafts
89-91 Peters Avenue
Mulgrave
Victoria 3170

DMC Needlecraft Pty
PO Box 317
Earlswood 2206
New South Wales 2204

Ireland Needlecraft Pty Ltd
2-4 Keppel Drive
Hallam
Victoria 3803

New Zealand

The Embroidery Shop
Greville-Parker
286 Queen Street
Masterton

The Embroiderer
142a Hinemoa Street
Birkenhead
Auckland

Broomfields
16 Merivale Mall
Christchurch

USA

Anne Brinkley Designs Inc
761 Palmer Avenue
Holmdel
NJ 97733

The DMC Corporation
Port Kearney Boulevard
#10 South Kearney
NJ 07032

Gay Bowles Sales Inc
PO Box 1060
Janesville
WI 53547

Appleton Brothers of London
West Main Road
Little Compton
RI 02837

Threadbenders
2260 Como Avenue
St Paul
MI 55108

Potpourri Etc
PO Box 78
Redondo Beach
CA 90277

Coats and Clarks
Susan Bates Inc
30 Patewood Drive
Greenville
SC 29615

Paterna
JCA Inc
35 Scales Lane
Townsend
MA 01469

The Thread Connection
1020 East Carson Street
Pittsburgh
PA 15203

In Stitches
10611 Abercorn Extension
Savannah
GA 31419

Kemp's Krafts
5940 Taylor St
Coloma
MI 49038

Cross Stitched Miracles
PO Box 32282
Euclid
OH 44132

Count'n'Caboodle
Rt.2 PO Box 58
Elgin
ND 58533

Homestead Designs Inc
PO Box 1058
Bellingham
WA 98227

Daisy Chain
PO Box 1258
Parkersburg
WV 26102

Bettekaril's Needlecrafts
PO Box 5008
Brandon
MS 39047

Mary Jane's Cross'n'Stitch Inc
5120 Belmont Road
Downer's Grove
IL 60515

Marilyn's Needlework
and Frames
4336 Plainfield Ave NE
Grand Rapids
MI 49505

Cross Creek
5131 Industrial Blvd
Maple Plain
MN 55359

Canada

Danish Art Needlework
PO Box 442
Lethbridge
Alberta

Dick and Jane
2352 West 41st Avenue
Vancouver
British Columbia

South Africa

S A Threads and Cottons Ltd
43 Somerset Road
Cape Town

Japan

Sanyei Imports
PO Box 5
Hashima Shi
Gifu 501-62